Georg Kugler

The Lipizzans

A guide for visitors
of the Spanish Riding School and the
Lipizzan Museum

Pichler Verlag

Introduction

THE HORSE, OUR COMPANION

The horse as our companion, the companion of both the war hero as well as the prince of peace, is often vaunted, its praises sung. An English saying says: "The world would be nothing without man, but man would be nothing without the horse." The taming of the wild horse has to be one of the most important achievements of the Neolithic people. The horse became a domestic animal, an animal whose capacity for work became the measure of all power. Not until centuries later through its use as work animal were its invaluable capabilities as a saddle and coach horse recognised.

Without the saddle horse world history would have taken a different course entirely; it would have been impossible, for example, for Alexander the Great to create his vast empire, nor would the conquering strides of the Mongolian cavalry, such as the one under Genghis Khan, have had such an impact. Only over water were humans able to travel greater distances with less effort.

In Central Asia small, tough saddle horses, large, strong draft horses and agile, light hunting horses were bred. It was probably the Hyksos who brought the horses to Egypt around 1650 B.C; from here they spread to the Mediterranean coasts, but this was not the only way that the horse came to Europe.

The Greeks are known as the founders of classical equitation. The oldest preserved treatise was written by the cavalry officer and historian Xenophon from Athens. Written in about 400 B.C., it is based on ancient but lost scripts. It wasn't until 2000 years later that Xenophon's textbook on cavalry found its successor in Neapolitan Federico Grisone's *Gli ordini di cavalcare (The Rules of Equitation*, 1550). For Grisone riding was an art belonging to the much admired ancient world, which he believed needed a renaissance as much as ancient literature, architecture and sculpture.

The "Eastern horse" of Ancient Egypt was taken over by the Bedouin nomads after the breakdown of the high cultures and have been bred as pure Arabians since Mohammed. During the course of the 7th century B.C. followers of the Prophet Mohammed also conquered the countries around the north-African Mediterranean coast and encountered the wild horse of the Berber people in the Atlas mountains and in Spain with the Iberian breed of horse, which the Romans used in ceremonies.

In the early 8th century the Arab warriors conquered the southern Iberian peninsular and founded an empire with centres in Cordoba, Seville and Granada. They cultivated a high culture like no other known in the largely barbarian Europe. Beautiful Arabian horses were part of the opulence of this society but a new breed of horse was created by the Caliphs, which exhibited extraordinary beauty and intelligence through the cross-breeding of Arabians, Barbs and Iberians.

Due to its outstanding and stable disposition, the Arabian and also the Spanish Arabian have been cross-bred with almost all of the European horse breeds. The versatility of the European horse was established in ancient times and increased due to selective breeding and natural selection influenced by the environment and territory.

Above: A rider from the Parthenon frieze on the Acropolis in Athens, marble relief Phidias school, 2nd half of the 5th century BC – London, British Museum
Left page: Portrait of a Lipizzaner mare in Piber
Page 2/3: Morning training in the riding school: *Capriole* on the rein.

The Lipizzans

ANCESTRY AND BREEDING

From 1580 onwards, under the reign of Archduke Charles of Inner Austria, the youngest brother of Emperor Maximilian II, Lipizzan horses had been bred at the Austrian imperial stud farm in Karst near Trieste. Charles had purchased the small stud Lipizza (Lipica) sitting high above the Adria from the archbishop of Trieste with the intention of breeding horses for the "Spanish" cavalry and hunting horses. The Andalusians were purchased yearly in Spain and cross-bred with Neapolitans and horses from the Italian Polesine region which were highly appreciated by the Duke of Mantua.

For a long time these horses were called "Spanish Karsts" or simply "Karst" horses. It wasn't until the latter half of the 18th century that they were named after the stud farm, using the Italian name "Lippiza".

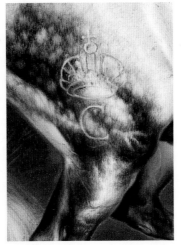

Archduke Charles followed the example of the Italian Renaissance princes, who were in need of a light yet powerful horse for the their luxurious life in the newly built residencies and villas in the country. This was the Spanish-Neapolitan cross. The Arabian full-blood was a beautiful saddle horse but not suitable as a coach horse and also not up to the demands of the cavalry. The new art of equitation began to spread throughout Europe, as did horse breeding, and the Lipizzans could be considered the most noble fruits of this trend. But there were other Habsburg studs that had similar goals. Maria of Hungary, a sister of Charles V, had already brought Spanish-Neapolitan horses to her stud in western Hungary (today Burgenland). She bequeathed them to her nephew, Emperor Maximilian II, who, as Charles V's son-in-law was obligated to the Spanish-Burgundian culture, created riding stables for his horses in the *Stallburg* in 1572 in Vienna. As King of Bohemia he purchased a stud in Kladruby on the river Elbe, where "Spanish" horses of the same blood line were bred, like the "Karsts". They were not only used for hunting and in tournaments but were also ideal as coach horses to pull the new type of Hungarian carriage that was fashionable at the time.

The Habsburgs had long been connected politically and culturally with their neighbouring country, the Kingdom of Hungary. Forming a union between the Danube countries and their southern and northern neighbouring countries had long been a political target. This amalgamation was made possible by Ferdinand I of Austria, who had also reigned as King of Bohemia and Hungary since 1526. The new coach was brought to Central Europe through his Vienna court and became popular as the imperial coach. It is thought to have been built in the west-Hungarian city of Kocs, hence the name in all European languages. And so it could be said that the Imperial House of Austria was responsible for two of the most luxurious phenomena of modern civilization: the saddle horse, and the coach and its elegant team.

The "Spanish" horse has a special place in the history of horse breeding, not least due to its ancestry being traceable back over centuries without interruption. Through its collected power it resembles a Baroque work of art, frugal and powerful, spirited and patient. The Lipizzan is everything but a modern sport horse. As mentioned earlier, the ancestors of today's Lipizzans didn't only come from Andalusia, Naples and the Polesina in Northern Italy, but also from court studs with Spanish horses in Germany (Lippe) and Denmark (Frederiksbørg) as

Above: Emperor Charles VI's monogramme, a C with the imperial crown, the stud brand on the right thigh of a Kladruby Apple White stallion. Detail from a painting by Johann Georg von Hamilton, 1722. (compare with picture on page 10)

Left page: The imperial Lipizza stud in Karst. Detail of a painting by Johann Georg von Hamilton, 1727.

well as directly from Arabia. Lipizzan horses were bred to the Kladruby stock from the Bohemian court stud farm and crossed again with related blood. The following Spanish-Neapolitan stallions are the foundation sires of the Lipizzan breed: Pluto, Conversano, Favory, Neapolitano and Maestoso.

In 1826 it was decided that the oriental stallion Siglavy would be made available as the sixth foundation stallion. Field marshal Prince Charles Philipp of Schwarzenberg had brought Siglavy with him from France after the victory over Napoleon and made him available to the *Oberststallmeisteramt* (Master of the Stables authority). Thus today there are six stallion families whose lines stem from the following sires:

Pluto: White horse from the Danish Royal stud farm in Frederiksborg, pure Spanish origins, born 1765.
Conversano: Dark brown/black, Neapolitan, born 1767.
Favory: Dun (mouse grey), Spansh Karst from the imperial stud farm in Kladruby, born 1779.
Neapolitano: Bay Neapolitan from Polesina, born 1790.
Siglavy: White, pure-blooded Arabian, born 1810 in Syria, belonged to Prince Schwarzenberg and purchased in 1826 for the imperial stud farm in Lipizza.
Maestoso: White, father, a pure-blooded Neapolitan, mother, pure-blooded Spanish dam, born at the imperial military stud in Mezöhegyes (Hungary) in 1819, and sired by a stallion of the same name born in 1773 in Kladruby.

Lipizzan mares also descend from these stallion lines (as their branding shows) or from special broodmare lines that each descend from a foundation dam. In Piber today there are still 18 foundation mare families:
Sardinia and **Spadiglia** (Karsts), **Stornella** and **Famosa** (from Kopcany, Slovakia), **Africa**, **Almerina**, **Englanderia**, **Presciana** and **Europa** (from Kladruby), **Deflorata** (from Denmark) and the Arabian mare families **Gidrane**, **Djebrin**, **Mercurio**, the Croatian families **Elien**, **Miss Wood**, **Hamad Flora** (from Vukovar), **Theodorosta** (from Bukovina), **Rava** (from Kladruby).

Above: Néput, an Apple White horse cantering. Painting by Johann Georg von Hamilton, ca. 1720.
Right: Branding symbol of the stallions (above) and of the mares (below) of the six foundation stallions.

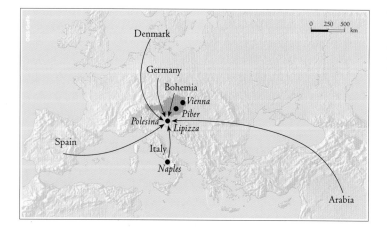

THE IMPERIAL HORSE

As well as the "Spanish Karsts" of the court stud farm in Lipizza/Lipica other studs had Andalusian-Neapolitan horses. In the court stud in Kladruby robust carriage horses, so-called *Karossiers* of the same ancestry, were bred for the Baroque festive carriages. Bred to the Karst on the other hand were saddle horses for hunting, which were at first only delivered to the archducal court of the Habsburg sovereign of Inner Austria in Graz. When Archduke Ferdinand of Inner Austria as the oldest of the Habsburg dynasty became emperor (he reigned as Ferdinand II from 1619–1637), he moved to Vienna and dissolved the royal household in Graz. The Karst court stud thus became "imperial" and from then on the famous horses, despite the great distance, were transferred to the Vienna court. In the riding school there they were trained by excellent Spanish and Italian riding teachers. The stables, riding school and stud were the pride and joy of every Baroque princely house. The emperors Leopold I (1658–1705), Joseph I (1705–1711) and Charles VI (1711–1740), also later his daughter Maria Theresia (Queen of Hungary, Archduchess of Austria 1740–1780) all loved horses and took a personal interest in the stables, schools, and stud farms.

New court stables were commissioned by Charles VI from 1719 to be built by court architect Johann Bernhard Fischer von Erlach. Now 600 horses, the carriage house, the saddle, harness and tack rooms and the magnificent service apartment of the stable master were all under one roof.

The imperial breeding facilities, which also included one

Above: Birds' eye view of Emperor Charles VI's Royal and Imperial court stables after its expansion by Emperor Franz Joseph. Coloured lithography by Vinzenz Katzler, after 1854.
Left above: Cerbero, a Neapolitan Porcelain doing a *capriole*. Painting by Johann Georg von Hamilton, 1721.
Left below: Scaramuz, a Kladruby Apple White horse doing a *piaffe* on the rein. Painting by Johann Georg von Hamilton, 1722.
Next double page: A White Stallion from Karst in a magnificent saddle on the rein. Painting by Johann Georg von Hamilton, ca. 1720.

in the west-Hungarian Schloss Halbthurn since 1717, expanded to a size that had never been equalled before (or thereafter). Charles VI commissioned his court painter Johann Georg von Hamilton, a specialist in painting horses, to paint landscapes of the stud farms and portraits of his favourite horses. Maria Theresia collected more than 25 of these paintings in a room created especially for this purpose, the so-called Rösselzimmer in Schloss Schönbrunn. Five more of Hamilton's horse paintings are exhibited in the Lipizzan Museum.

These paintings (see p. 6 and 10) show the remarkable colours of the Spanish horses' coats. They were given imaginative names: *Dappled Porcelains, Tiger Caparisons, Lizards, Isabelline, Ice Whites, Apple Whites, Grey Whites, and Trout Whites.* The so-called *Vienna Ermine*, with light grey skin and shimmering gold hair, and white-coloured mane and tail hair, was particularly admired.

Like all white or grey horses, Lipizzan foals are dark brown or almost black at birth; the coat then lightens with each season. Most dark colts become pure white between six and ten years of age.

At the beginning of the 19th century, after the English fashion, white horses were preferred, and attempts were made to strengthen the genetic dominance of the white coat through Arabian blood. Through the oriental white horse Siglavy even a new stallion line was established. Today Lipizzans are considered the white horse *par excellence*, but traditionally a dark brown stallion is always included in the Riding School's shows.

The foals stay in the pen with their mothers for about half a year, after which they are weaned and receive the four brands at the stud farm: The stud brand 'P' on the left croup with the Austrian imperial crown; the 'L' which stands for a pure-bred Lipizzan on the left cheek; the ancestral brand on the left withers identifying the stallion line of the sire and mare family of the dam; and the foal registry number behind the right withers. The foals are given a double name – that of the sire and that of the dam; the mares carry only the mother's name.

After the colts have spent at least three summers in the pastures they undergo a strict physical examination. Only the ones in excellent health are sent to the Spanish Riding School for training because tradition so dictates: since the 18th century the Lipizzan is one of the best schooled horses in the world – intelligent, quick to learn, and having a natural talent for the classical gaits of the Haute École, both for the Airs on the Ground and Airs Above the Ground.

The Lipizzans were appreciated for their "personalities" with particular talents and were not simply "painted" but "portraited"! It is said of the skewbald Cerbero, whose portrait by Hamilton hangs in the museum, that he was "a truly excellent jumper".

Although the training at the Vienna Riding School was strictly in the hands of Spanish or Italian trainers, it was based on the work of French masters – brought to perfection by La Guérinière (1688–1751) who drew from works by Antoine Pluvinel. It wasn't until the reign of the Baroque Emperor Joseph I and Charles VI that the Viennese Chief Riders Johann Christoph von Regenthal and Adam von Weyrother achieved European fame in their own right.

The imperial riding school took its leading role, however, under Max von Weyrother, who worked in Vienna from 1815 until 1835, and from 1825 as Chief Rider. Strictly following La Guérinière, Weyrother refined his theories and combined them with his own personal experience.

Weyrother's approach is characterised by a motto that will comfort visitors to the Lipizzan Museum shuddering at the sight of the earlier used curbs and snaffles from the last century: "The more iron in the horses mouth, the less competent the rider". Weyrother's teachings circulated throughout Europe through his students and are still treasured and followed today at the Spanish Riding School.

As the 19th century was the age of science and medicine, the breeding of horses and everything related to it was systematically and scientifically researched. Hippology became a science, which even the old court studs had to abide by. The studies by animal painter Franz O'Stückenberg exhibited in the Lipizzan Museum are testimony to the inventory done at Lipizza according to the dictates of hippology as authorised by the Superintendent's Office (Oberststallmeisteramt) in 1897.

All the same, the exclusive riding school and the court studs outside of Vienna were almost unknown to the public. Rather, the Lippizans were known to one-and-all as the carriage horses of the court and were admiringly dubbed "white imperial horses". Roughly 200 Lipizzans were kept in the court stables for the light, elegant coaches that were used for daily jaunts during Emperor Franz Josef's time.

THE STUD FARMS: LIPPIZA

When Archduke Charles purchased a small farm high above Trieste in the Karst mountains in 1580 to build a stud farm, he followed the example of his brother, Emperor Maximilian II, who had built one there for his imperial court in Prague in Kladruby on the river Elbe in 1562. From 1564 onwards Archduke Charles had reigned from Graz over Styria, Carinthia and Carniola, Istria and the Austrian Littoral, Gorizia and Trieste since 1564. At this time most of these countries had already been governed by the House of Hapsburg for about 200 years.

Once the stud facility had been built, the horses from Polesina (Rovigo region), which was not far away, and also from Spain were purchased for breeding. The imperial ambassador in Spain, Hans Christoph von Khevenhüller, proved to be a prudent buyer. In a cost report from November 1581 there are six stallions listed, which were transported to the archduke for the first time.

More than 300 years later the directorate of the stud farm commemorated the founding with a plaque on a stables building:

"The widely-travelled Archduke Charles, who founded the Karst stud farm on the rocky Trieste territory, undoubtedly took as his model the rigorous manner in which the Arabian horse, which despite frugal fodder and privations of every type, is endowed with strength and tenacity. The magnificent Lipizzan horses that have been raised on the stony pastures of Lippiza and the high mountain pastures of Prestranegg are testament to the regent's foresight as regarding the breeding of horses in his country."

Hans Christoph von Khevenhüller was an ambassador to Emperor Rudolph II, buying not only artworks in Spain but also horses, year after year. It is said that Rudolph II had 3000 paintings in his gallery, and in his studs and stables, 3000 Horses! Emperor Rudolph II and his successor Matthias remained childless. In 1619 the Styrian Archduke Ferdinand succeeded Matthias and unified the Inner Austrian countries with all the territories of the main Austrian line. From this point onwards the director of the imperial stables in Vienna also became head of the stud farm in Karst.

Through Charles VI the stud increased greatly in size with the purchase of the locations Adelsberg and Prestranegg. At that time in Lippiza alone there were about 150 broodmares. A painting by Hamilton (see p. 6) shows a herd on a stony pasture, and an anonymous painting (see p. 16) portrays a stud building in the middle of the mountainous Karst landscape.

During the Napoleon wars the Lipizzan horses had to be evacuated three times (1797, 1805 and 1809) to escape from the French army. The third evacuation was the worst. About 300 horses were underway for six weeks and when they finally arrived on the river Maros in Hungary a catastrophe occurred: a quarter of the broodmares gave birth to dead foals.

Lippiza, Trieste and the Austrian Littoral as part of the province of Illyria were ceded to France. The studs degenerated, the inventory was lost, the forests that had been so painstakingly planted were cut down. The horses stayed in Hungary until 1815, after the victory over Napoleon, when they were moved to Lippiza again. And the whole process had to be started from the beginning. The stallion Maestoso was procured from the Mezöhegyos stud farm and the Arab Siglavy from Prince Schwarzenberg. Due to the unfortunate circumstances, Emperor Franz ordered that the stud farm registries be kept in duplicate.

The stud farm, however, was in danger once again. Because of the Napoleonic wars the military strategy was subject to fundamental changes. The training of the modern cavalry was no longer possible without Haute École. There was talk of closing both the court stud farm and the Spanish Riding School, but in the end the idea

Above: Duke Charles II, founder of the Karst imperial stud in Lippiza, with a hunting dog. Painter unknown, ca. 1580.
Left page: Siglavy-Traga, a cross-bred Karst white stallion. Gouache by Franz O'Stückenberg, Lippiza, 1897.

was rejected. But it was Emperor Franz Joseph who decided to keep the Lipizzans; in 1850 he allocated the necessary funds for a generous reconstruction of the stud farm and thus facilitated the continuation of the breeding. In 1894 the number of horses at the Karst imperial stud farm had risen to 300, with about 250 dressage and carriage horses in Vienna.

During the First World War, following Italy's decision in May 1915 to join Austria's allies, the broodmares and foals were evacuated from Lippiza to Laxenburg near Vienna and to Kladruby near Prague. Following the defeat, the Austrian Littoral and Trieste and thereby Karst ceded to the kingdom of Italy, the Lipizzan stallions in Kladruby and the foals in Czechoslovakia were seized, and the horses from Laxenburg were turned over to Italy. Only 97 stallions and foals, which were kept at the Federal Stud Farm in Piber, Styria, remained the property of the Republic of Austria.

Barely 25 years later, during the final stages of the Second World War, Yugoslavian partisans occupied the Italian border region around Trieste. Lippiza/Lipica was taken over by the new communist Yugoslavia, which rebuilt the farm with Lipizzans expropriated from the stud farms of the Austro-Hungarian aristocracy and other confiscated horses. A few years later the stud farm was closed and then – at the behest of Tito, head of state – opened again. It has been a Slovenian federal stud farm since 1989.

Above: Coach driveway to the Karst imperial stud in Lippiza. Photo, ca. 1890.
Centre and below: Herd of mares at the Karst imperial stud, Lippiza. Photo, ca. 1890.
Left page: The Karst imperial stud in Lippiza. Painter unknown, ca. 1770

THE STUD FARMS: PIBER

The idyllically-situated Austrian federal stud farm in Piber has been the home of the Lipizzans since 1920, if only with a small part of what remained of the stock after the peace treaty of St. Germain and the founding of the new Republic of German-Austria came into effect. The stallions from the riding school in Vienna were kept in Austria as a guarantee for further breeding for they had been left untouched by the division in Italy. The stud farm building is a Baroque castle that was built by the Benedictine monks of the St. Lambrecht monastery as their estate and forestation administration centre. Emperor Joseph II expropriated the assets during the course of the reform and had it remodelled as a military stud. Situated in the southern Styrian mountains, the site couldn't offer the mares and foals the same conditions found in the harsh environment of the Karst mountains, but the horses adapted quickly to their surroundings. The climate and food quality were roughly the same in Piber as in Karst, and thanks to strict breeding practices, the Lipizzans survived as a race.

Summer in alpine pastures is extremely important for the upbringing of the foals. There the craggy ground and the harsh climate represent similar conditions to their homeland. The young Lipizzans develop their natural gait in harmony with nature and learn the essential sure-footedness. Each colt must spend three summers in these pastures before it is transferred to the Spanish Riding School, after a very careful selection process. The young stallions are subject to various challenges to see whether they are suitable to be trained as an Haute École dressage horse.

The succeeding countries of the Austro-Hungarian monarchy also continued to breed Lipizzans after the First World War. Following Austria's annexation to Fascist Germany, the new, small state of Austria became a province and the Spanish Riding School was handed over to the German Wehrmacht. The Lipizzans were moved from Piber to a central military stud farm in Hostau in 1942. In April 1945 American troops moved the horses from there to Bavaria, and, more than a decade later, they returned to Styria from Upper Austria.

Left, above and centre: The Baroque castle Piber, exterior and inner courtyard
Left below: Lipizzaner stallion in Piber, in the background the castle church.
Left page above: The Propstei in Piber. Tapestry by Georg Matthäus Vischer, ca. 1680/90.
Left page below: Mares and foals at Piber

Piber, the home of the Austrian Lipizzans. Mares with their foals. Colts on the high mountain pastures.
Centre left: The Piber stud brand, a "P" with the imperial crown.

The Haute École

THE PERFECT HORSEMAN

Humanistic scholars and artists of the Renaissance dedicated a special interest to nature, to its study, research and presentation. Beautiful and rare objects became collectors' items, making up compendiums with other precious objects after having been in some way reworked by man. Nature began to be considered part of the human living environment, and the parks surrounding the princely castles are examples of man's endeavour to establish spiritual and artistic dominion over nature. Wild-life parks containing red deer, camels or antelopes and also exotic birds were part of almost every castle.

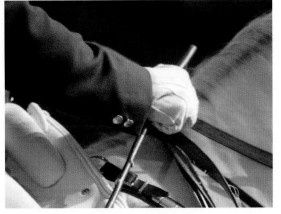

In this milieu, saddle and carriage horses took on great significance. Great care was taken to ennoble their characteristics through selective breeding and to train them to full capacity; stables and riding schools were constructed that were as luxurious as any palace.

Training the horses in the lessons of the so-called Haute École was considered the highest achievement of dressage. It is an exercise in the perfection of the horse's natural talents to such a degree that it resembles a work of art. It is also about training the rider, who must have command over the capabilities of his mount and be able to use them to prove himself in tournaments and in battle, to achieve absolute synchronicity with others in parades and to distinguish himself in the riding school and at equestrian events.

The first modern riding academy was founded in Naples by Giovanni B. Pignatelli, who wrote a treatise on the art of riding in 1552, which reawakened an interest in the ancient traditions. His colleague, riding teacher Federico Griso, worked with him but more as a theoretician.

Pignatelli and Griso passed their knowledge on to three French riding masters of the 17th century: Antoine de Pluvinel, Salomon de La Broue and Chevalier de Saint-Antoine.

Pluvinel, who under King Henry IV was one of the most influential courtiers, was one of the founders of the classic Haute École. The principals for the lessons he gave to the Crown Prince Ludwig (XIII) can be found in the work *Instruction du Roi en l'art de monter à Cheval*. Pluvinel's training was "humane" compared to his Italian predecessors. He introduced the use of pillars and invented the cavesson nose halter for longeing.

In England William Cavendish, Duke of Newcastle, wrote articles about equitation in the second half of the 17th century. Because they were also published in Antwerp in French, they became standard throughout Europe.

One century later François Robichon de la Guérinière reformed Pluvinel's highly stylised riding theory and also that of the Duke of Newcastle. Guérinière was Louis XV's stable master and can be described as the greatest riding master of the 18th century. He developed a new approach to equitation and created the basis of modern dressage. His influence is felt particularly in the Spanish Riding School in Vienna, where his shoulder-in technique (*L' Epaule en dedans*) remains the basis for the "Airs Above the Ground".

The most famous depictions of Haute École figures from this classic epoch are etchings by the painter and publisher Johann Elias Ridinger from Augsburg. His *Neue Reitschul, vorstellend einen vollkommenen Reuter in allen Lectionen*, a series of 18 etchings, appeared in 1734. A comparison with the images gathered today in the Spanish Riding School shows that the tradition of Haute École has remained unchanged. This comparison can be seen

Left page: Large quadrille at the closing of a performance at the Spanish Riding School

in projections shown at the Lipizzan Museum. Responsible for the training of the horses and also the éleves are and have always been the riders themselves. As masters and teachers they pass on their knowledge to the new generations.

The training begins with acquiring the perfect seat; it is as indispensable for imparting commands to the horse as it is for the overall picture of horse and rider ensemble. By riding the stallions trained thoroughly using Haute École methods, the young rider himself learns self-discipline and humility. To begin with, the rider learns from his horse; later, the trained rider then educates the young stallions through his hard and patient work.

Above: Ludwig XIII, king-to-be of France, in a *capriole*. Tapestry from the series "Riding Lessons", designed by Jacob Jordaens, Brussels, pre-1650.
Left page above: Two engravings from "The New School of Riding" by Johann Elias Ridinger, 1734.
Left page below: *Capriole* on the rein at the pillars. Engraving by Crispin de Pas from "Manège du Roi" by Antoine de Pluvinel, Paris 1623.

The training plan of the Spanish Riding School stems from the so-called *Directiven* that were documented in writing before 1900: The first stage of the Directives is learning the natural gaits, walking, trotting and galloping in straight lines. The second stage is the smooth and rhythmic execution of all gaits, turns and manoeuvres. These are the Airs on the Ground.

The third stage is training the horse to move in a raised upright position, in all its natural and artificial gaits. These are the Airs Above the Ground. Each gait should follow rhythmically and should never appear hurried or exhibit any uneven steps. The desirable characteristics in a dressage horse are:

Collection – Ideal carriage; centre of gravity shifted to the hindquarters, relieving of the forequarters, expressive, animated movement.

Contact – elastic, soft, constant link through the reins, between the rider's hand and the horse's mouth.

Lightness – lively, rhythmical movement, relaxed, flexible; natural head and tail posture.

The Training and Development of a Rider

Éleve: Admission between the ages of 15 and 16 years. Training on the school stallion on the longe. The éleve learns to be loose and relaxed, above all, however, he must learn an impeccable seat; proper grooming is also taught. If the student can present all the gaits and manoeuvres of the Haute École on the school stallion, he becomes a Riding Candidate.

Riding Candidate: Intensive riding instruction, always in conjunction with the training of the horse, by the responsible Rider and Chief Rider. The student is allocated his "own" horse and must train it.

If the candidate has fully trained a stallion to full maturity, he applies to become a Rider.

The training as an éleve and riding candidate takes about eight years.

Rider: A trained rider in Haute École both in airs on and above the ground who trains his own horses and takes part in individual parades and training as well as in the quadrille.

Chief Rider: Responsible for the training of the éleves and the Riding Candidates. He must be particularly well-versed in Airs Above the Ground.

First Chief Rider: Has full authority over the riding personnel, is responsible for the entire school operation and its representation in public.

Left page: School quadrille in the Winter Riding School. Rider's salutation at the end of a performance, shown in four different movements. Painting by Ludwig Koch, 1934.
Right: Aquarelle by Ludwig Koch from "Horsemanship in Pictures", 1929.
Upper Row: *Piaffe* at the pillars; school trot.
Centre row: School canter; school canter – *renvers* right
Bottom row: *Pirouette* right; *renvers* left on the long rein

AIRS ON THE GROUND

Shoulder-in – A side-ways walk away from the direction that the horse is moving; the inner fore-leg crosses over the outer leg. This movement is done in the walk, trot and canter.

The following side-ways walks are developed from the shoulder-in, but differentiate from it in that the two outer legs are placed over the inner two, and through the position of the horse's body to the wall.

Travers – Traversale (half-pass). "Haunches-in"; a forward and lateral movement whereby the horse's outside legs cross diagonally in front of the inside legs.

Renvers – A side-ways walk with the tail towards the wall rather than the head.

Passage – also Spanish trot. A trot with the highest "collection". A powerful but slow passage only under the rider. The horse swings from one diagonal pair of legs to the other and suspends each one a little longer than with a normal trot ("elevation"). The passage is an extension of the *piaffe*.

Piaffe – *A cadenced trot*, an artificial trot in one place with the rider or at the pillars, with an elastic but marked flexation of the joints; the fore-legs are lifted higher than the hind legs. The horse should stand straight without swaying or crossing its legs and still convey the impression of dancing.

Pirouette – A tight turn on the haunches, a shortened canter on the hind legs- an extension of the renvers canter. The horse makes a circle in six to eight regular cantering steps without moving away from its place; but it shouldn't turn on one spot. There is a difference between a half and full *pirouette*. The *pirouette* is one of the most elegant yet difficult movements because it needs to be executed rhythmically, fluidly and with perfect balance.

The horses at the Spanish Riding School present a special exhibition with an exercise on the **long rein**. The instructor stands near the horse's hindquarters while it performs all the exercises of the Airs on the Ground. Only a perfectly trained and obedient horse will respond to commands given with the reins alone.

Left page: Morning training in the Winter Riding School

Above left: *Passage*
Above right: Half *travers (Traversale)* to the right
Below: *Piaffe* at the pillars

Morning training in the Winter Riding School (from left): Stablemaster Prince Emerich Thurn and Taxis, a saddled horse animated to do a *capriole* at the pillars, a brown horse doing a *piaffe* on the rein, a *courbette* on the rider's rein, horse in a Spanish step on the rider's rein walking, a red horse cantering, a grey horse in a *pesade*. Painting by Julius von Blaas, 1890.

AIRS ABOVE THE GROUND

Levade – The horse rises on its hindquarters to an angle not higher than 45°, and calmly remains in this position for several seconds. The *levade* can be performed alone by the horse at the pillars or with the rider. A series of repeated *levades* is called a *mézair or terre à terre*.

Pesade – Similar to the levade. The rise on the haunches is more shallow, but higher than 45°.

Croupade – The horse jumps out of the *levade* in a position similar to the *pesade* and keeps his hind legs tucked tightly underneath it so as not to reach a horizontal stretch. This movement precedes the *courbette* and the *capriole*.

Courbette – The horse jumps 2 to 5 times out of the *levade* without lowering his fore-legs. It is one of the most difficult jumps, and it often takes years until a horse is discovered that is talented in the *courbette*. The *courbette* is also extremely difficult for the rider.

Ballotade – Precedes the *capriole*, similar to the *croupade*, in which the horse kicks out his tightly gathered hind legs; from behind the horse shoes are visible. Through the leap off the ground the horse is almost stretched horizontally.

Capriole – The horse makes a vertical leap into the air from the *piaffe* with all four legs and kicks (stretches) out its hind legs almost simultaneously so that its body is horizontal. This the most impressive Haute École movement learned only by especially talented horses at the pillars (see p. 30). The *capriole* demands great concentration also from the riders; as with all the Haute École jumps, he rides without stirrups.

A show at the Spanish Riding School concludes with the *grand quadrille* and is performed in perfect harmony. The quadrille was part of the tradition of the great court carousel. Initially, prior to the fall of the monarchy, it was performed by four horses, as shown in the painting from 1932 by the important horse painter Ludwig Koch (see p. 26). The legendary head of the Riding School, Colonel Podhajsky, developed the quadrille to incorporate eight stallions in the Forties. On special occasions and when there is enough room, the quadrille can also be performed by 12 horses.

Morning training in the Winter Riding School. In the foreground: *Levade*

Above left: *Levade.* **Above right:** *Courbette* on the rein. **Below:** *Capriole* on the rein

The Lipizzans' Stage

THE STALLBURG

In 1560 Emperor Ferdinand I began the construction of a large building in the east of the old Hofburg, which was to be the residence of his son Maximilian II; after more than 30 years in Spain the young archduke was returning to Austria. At his spectacular arrival he brought with him not only the legendary elephant and other exotic animals but also numerous Andalusian horses, for which, after his father's death, he had stables built on the ground floor (1564). Thereafter it was called the Stallburg (Imperial Stables). He himself moved to the Hofburg.

The arcades of the inner courtyard were later filled in to make room for the imperial painting gallery, which didn't move to the Upper Belvedere until 1778. It wasn't until after the Second World War that the arcades on the top floor were opened again. On the ground floor they are glassed in and are used by the Spanish Riding School and the Lipizzan Museum.

In 1744 Maria Theresia had a court pharmacy built in the north wing of the Stallburg, which was closed in 1995 and became part of the Lipizzan Museum in 1997. The Baroque furniture of the pharmacy was reserved and kept, while in other rooms, particularly in the cellar, huge reconstruction was necessary. Two rooms were given back to the Spanish Riding School. After the Second World War, during the time that the Lipizzans weren't in Vienna, they were used by the court pharmacy as a depot.

Above: Inner courtyard of the stables. School horses at morning training.
Left page: *Levade*

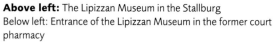

Above left: The Lipizzan Museum in the Stallburg
Below left: Entrance of the Lipizzan Museum in the former court pharmacy
Above right: Inner courtyard of the Stallburg
Centre right: Horse solarium and plaiting the tails
Below right: Saddle storeroom

THE WINTER RIDING SCHOOL

Spain, a country with a history of classical riding and horse breeding, had been ruled by the Habsburgs since the 15th century. Since Emperor Charles V, the old Spanish line of the Royal House of Austria had ruled half the world. For this reason Spain was a role model for the young German line that ruled the Holy Roman Empire of the German Nation. The Habsburg princes resided in the capital cities of their respective countries – Prague, Vienna, Graz and Innsbruck – and had stables and riding schools built for the highly appreciated Spanish horses.

Thanks to the military exploits of Prince Eugene during his youth, Emperor Charles VI (1685–1740) periodically tried to become the contracted air to the Spanish throne – successfully – and reigned as King Charles III of Spain from 1703 to 1711. Following the death of his brother, Emperor Joseph I, Charles finally had to give up his dream of the Spanish empire in order to take over the emperor's throne in Germany. Despite this, he held on to many Spanish practices and traditions, particularly in that many of his Spanish devotees followed him to Vienna. The appreciation for Spanish horses is an expression of this position. His goal was to re-evaluate the Vienna Riding School, which Emperor Maximilian II had founded in 1565 as a necessary part of the Spanish riding stables.

Charles then had a new Winter Riding School built, which was part of a comprehensive construction programme that was meant to restructure the Hofburg according to the needs of an absolute prince based on the Baroque model.

The emperor had well-known architects draw up plans, planned and constructed the court stables, the library, the summer castle Favorita, the completion of the entertainment castle and hunting castle and a monastery residence in Klosterneuburg more or less concurrently.

In 1729 Joseph Emanuel, the younger Fischer von Erlach, presented plans for the Winter Riding School,

Michaelerplatz.
Left, the court church St. Michael, in the centre of the Winter Riding School. Right, the old Burgtheater. Coloured engraving by Carl Schütz, 1784.

construction of which was carried out in just under six years. Construction of a cupola on Michaelerplatz was halted due to the positioning of the former Burgtheater. Nobody wanted to demolish it and thus the new Hofburg remained unfinished until the late 19th century. Numerous views of the Winter Riding School on Michaelerplatz with its corner stone dome show us the strange state of this half-completed façade. The riding hall with its two-story, circumferential gallery is an architectural masterpiece. Although the measurements of the arena (55 x 18 m and height of 17 m) are unusual, all the elements of the Baroque structure present a picture of absolute harmony. The column architecture on the long sides is representative of a temple-like court box on the narrow side, where a riding portrait of Charles VI is all the more impressive for its being the only colourful piece in the room. The portrait is by Johann Gottfried Auerbach; the horse – a real Spanish Karst – is the work of Johann Georg Hamilton.

The school strictly observes traditions, which must always be practiced. These include saluting the portrait of the builder when entering the arena or when beginning to work as a symbol of appreciation for having the fortune to ride in such a magnificent arena. After work is finished the dismounted student salutes his teacher. In former times both teacher and student would give their show of respect to the director of the riding school

before leaving the arena if he was a rider himself. In the centre of the arena are the two pillars, which are only used for training in Vienna and in the cavalry school in Saumur. In general Pluvinel is acknowledged as the founder of the pillars but he probably had role models that stemmed from ancient times. In any case he constantly used the pillars, the necessity of which is controversial today – some see them as only a relic of tradition. They serve to keep the horse in one place, only give him limited space and quasi limit it to the width of its legs, which is only important for the *piaffe* in Haute École. Older trainers say that by working at the pillars a horse can prove its talent and ability for the mastering of the Haute École jumps.

Above left: Picture of Emperor Charles VI riding, court balcony of the Winter Riding School. Painting by Johann Georg von Hamilton and Johann Gottfried Auerbach, ca. 1735.
Above right: "The Imperial and Royal riding track in the Burg". Title tapestry from the book by C. Klatte, Vienna, 1810.
Right page: The Winter Riding School from the visitor's gallery (above); Morning training (below).

THE CARROUSEL

Emperor Charles VI did not only intend the Winter Riding School to be used for training the horses from his stables but also for the training of the aristocratic youth and for court fêtes in general, with or without horses. In this respect the school was the venue for numerous different fêtes and events throughout the centuries. Some of them were of such pomp and circumstance the likes of which today are almost unthinkable. Some of these events included the carrousel, tilting at the rings and the "jousts" against Moor figures, which were popular with the riders and spectators alike.

The carrousel evolved from the medieval tournaments in which also women and children could take part – in central Europe the sleighs were particularly popular. Artistically carved, colourfully painted sleighs were staple possessions in all wealthy households. Even the children, the boys mostly as page-boys, had to practice this craft and, as it was two centuries before, it was taken for granted that one could take part in the carrousel. The horse plays an important role in the event because the carrousels were either ridden or drawn. Courses were laid for the carrousel, which took place outdoors along decorated pathways and parks, around fountains and bridges. Competitions were also staged indoors, where particular skill was needed. The jousts employed lances, swords or pistols, which were thrust against Negro or Turk figures and included tilting at the rings without leaving one's lane or making mistakes on the course. For the carrousel, coaches or sleighs were decorated with silver or gold-embroidered velvet cloths, and the horse's mane and tail was decorated with ribbons and tassels. The ladies and their "champions" dressed in matching colours. For the public carrousels on squares and city streets, couples' names were drawn a few weeks before the event so that they had ample time to prepare their entries and costumes.

These public events were publicised through flyers and advertisements in newspapers and always attracted crowds of spectators, who were critical judges of the riders' abilities, and applauded the extravagant costumes of the women. The fêtes were accompanied by live music.

Traditionally, the Vienna court carrousels took place in the Winter Riding School. A large painting by Martin van Meytens in Schloss Schönbrunn depicts one of the first carrousels, a "Ladies' Carousel". The 25 year-old Maria Theresia, then Queen of Hungary, held the event on 2nd January 1743 to celebrate the withdrawal of the French and Bavarians from Bohemia after the First Slesian War. Several young women are sitting in eight decorated coaches driven by men; the men are following the assigned lanes and the ladies are holding the lance. At the same time eight women, directed by the queen, are riding a quadrille.

In the following year the riding arena was turned into a ballroom, where a masked ball was held after the wedding of Archduchess Maria Anna, Maria Theresia's younger sister, and Prince Charles of Lorraine. One-hundred-and-thirty chandeliers and 52 huge mirrors were installed in the hall! The imperial family and the court made their entrance before 8000 guests, with 60 horses and ladies dressed in identical costumes. A particularly impressive painting by Ignace Duvivier from that year (1780) illustrates the tilting at the Moors. Another out-of-the-ordinary fête held in the hall was the presentation of the flying machine invented by Jakob Degen in April 1808.

During the Vienna Congress of 1814/15 the hall was the venue for huge parties, carrousels and masked balls for which the riding arena was transformed into a palm house, an orangery and a concert hall. One of the great musical events to be held in the Winter Riding School

Above: Empress Maria Theresia's carousel coach, 1743. Schönbrunn, Wagenburg.
Right page: Large "Moor Tapestry" in the Winter Riding School. Painting by Ignace Duvivier, 1780.
Page 42: Ladies' carrousel with eight shell coaches in the Winter Riding School on 2nd January 1743. Maria Theresia riding a quadrille on a "Lipizzan" with seven court ladies while her mother, the emperor's widow Elisabeth Christine, looks on from the imperial box against the backdrop of the equestrian portrait of Emperor Charles VI. Part of a painting by Martin van Meytens, from after 1765. Schloss Schönbrunn, Carrousel Room.

was the performance of Ludwig van Beethoven's Wellington's Victory conducted by the composer himself. In 1843 the 50th anniversary of Archduke Charles' receiving of the Maria Theresia military honour was celebrated with a carrousel organised by cavalry officers, which is depicted in a painting by Carl Goebels in the Lipizzan Museum and seems to have been a rather martial affair.

In 1830 the Winter Riding School was the venue for the first industrial products fair, and one year later, due to a cholera epidemic, even the stock exchange was moved there. And for decades the drawing of the state lottery took place here.

Politics followed economics. In July 1848, the year of the revolution, the Austrian parliament held its first session here. Visiting heads of state and important personal guests of the emperor not only had the honour of viewing performances of the riding school but were also spectators of the carrousel, the King of Prussia and the King of Belgium, no less, in 1853. Members of the court and the high aristocracy also took part in similar performances, as was the case with Maria Theresia's ladies' carousel – just like the last fête of this kind, which took place in April 1894. Two-hundred participants, including 125 riders in historical costume, gathered to honour the empress consort Elisabeth Christine at the celebration called by Emperor Franz Josef I, which included a mounted quadrille, carousels with two- and four-horse teams and traditional equestrian games, and an artillery parade.

THE LIPIZZANS AS COACH HORSES

The Lipizzans from the Karst Imperial Stud were not only highly valued as Baroque school horses behind the Hofburg walls, but also for pulling the imperial coaches in public. Almost 200 of these stallions were stabled in the imperial coach park, the Imperial & Royal Court Coach House (*k. u. k. Hofwagenburg*), which were part of the Imperial & Royal Court Stables controlled by the office of the *Oberststallmeister* (Master of the Imperial Stables), as were the studs and the riding schools, the various stables and the *Wagenburg*. The stable master presided over one of the four most important court positions – today comparable with the post of a minister- and was always granted to a member of highest aristocracy. The real director of the court stables, however, was the First Chief Rider. Until 1918 all these institutions were located in the imperial stables, which Emperor Karl VI had built between 1719 and 1729 and designed by Johann Bernhard Fischer von Erlach. Where the court stables once stood is today the Museum Quarter. In the central hall was the palace-like office of the stable master, and the stables attached to the side housed 400 horses. Lining the large inner courtyard where the coaches were yoked and the historical coaches and gala coaches presented and shown were the tack room, the workshop and storerooms. There was also a large riding school and stalls for the Campagne horses and the emperor's riding horses. It was the largest stables complex in the world, larger even than those in Versailles, but less grand than the Sultan's, whose magnificent horses ate out of silver troughs. Pompously outfitted were also both the oval stalls for the coach horses from the Kladruby imperial stud: 25 Spanish horses for the imperial coach and the large gala carriages and 25 black horses used for pulling the large coaches at funerals, cortèges and state processions.

The court stalls were divided accordingly: the oval stables for the Kladruby horses, the stables reserved for white coaches housed the Lipizzans and the stables for

Ceremonious entrance of Princess Isabella of Parma into Vienna as the bride of emperor-to-be Joseph II on 6th October 1760.
Schloss Schönbrunn, Ceremony Parlour.

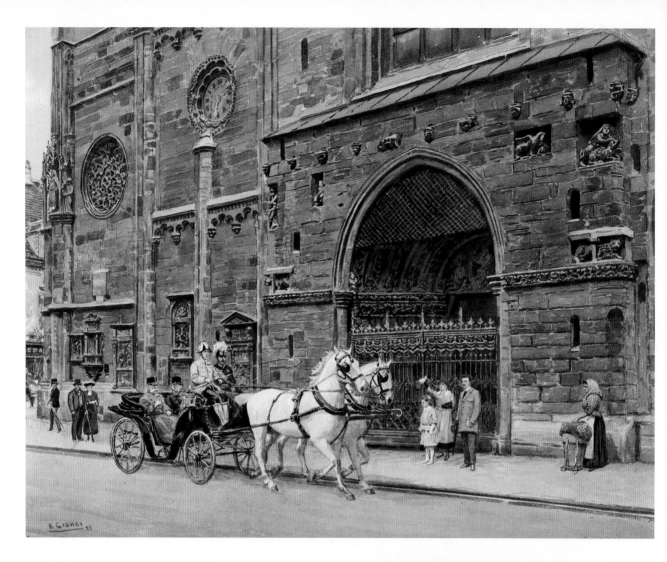

the English and Irish warm-
bloods, especially the Cleve-
land Bay, which were very
popular at the Vienna court,
but also the Furioso and Non-
ius stallions bred in Austria.
The stalls held up to 200 horses used for the city carriages,
coaches in the retinue and
also for the almost 100 coaches used by court officials on
business. The light coaches
pulled by the Lipizzans, so-
called *Jucker*, were employed
for every-day use, and were
driven at the imperial castles
outside of Vienna with Hungarian harnesses admired for
their proud gait and their
noble presence by the public,
and appreciated by the driv-
ers for their willingness and
obedience.

Above: Emperor Franz Joseph and his adjutant-General Count Eduard Paar in an open
"Mylord" drawn by Lipizzans in front of St. Stephan's cathedral. Gouache by Ernst Graner, 1911.
Below: Imperial coach outing with harnessed Lipizzans coming out of the Schweizertor of the Hofburg.
Aquarelle by Alexander Bensa, ca. 1850.

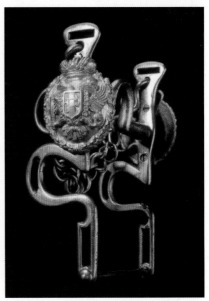

Above: Emperor Franz Joseph's state coach with eight Kladruby horses in gala harnesses in front of the Winter Riding School of the imperial stables. Photo, ca. 1895.
Below: Gala headgear, ca. 1890 (left); stirrups, ca. 1820 (centre); Harness piece with coat of arms, ca. 1890 (right).

The Court Riding School after 1918

THE TAKEOVER OF THE SPANISH RIDING SCHOOL BY THE REPUBLIC OF AUSTRIA

Following the fall of the Austro-Hungarian monarchy the court stables were closed by Prince Nikolaus Palffy, the last Master of the Imperial Stables, and was handed over to the newly instated authority within a few years. Most of the coaches, almost 400 horses – half of them Lipizzan - and all saddle horses were sold or assigned to the offices of the new republic "Germany-Austria". The prevailing idea at the time seemed to be to dispense with anything that was associated with "imperial" or "of the court" and expose it to vandalism. Thanks to the optimism of the administrators liquidating the imperial estate, in particular Baron Beck von Managetta and the former Chief Stable Master, Graf Rudolf van der Straten, about 50 historically and artistically precious coaches and sledges were given to the Kunsthistorisches Museum collection, and the stallions from the riding school were kept and not sold. As previously mentioned, the Lipizzan mares from the Karst imperial stud, which were partly evacuated to the court stud farm in Kladruby, Bohemia, and partly to the Laxenburg castle in 1915, were distributed between Italy, the Czech Republic and Austria, parts of the former Austro-Hungarian empire. In November 1920 the small herd left in Austria was transferred to the federal stud in Piber, directed by the former veterinarian Dr. Besel.

The administration of the stud and of the riding school was passed to the Ministry of Agriculture. Luckily the general consensus was that the institution of the Spanish Riding school should remain upheld, and Rudolf van der Straten, was appointed as the first post-war director. He was faced with the difficult job of getting the institute now owned by the Republic to make a profit and also to convince the public of the immense historical and cultural value of the institute and its responsibility to preserve and cultivate this legacy for the world. The general economic difficulties, inflation and unemployment created problems for the new director, and only slowly could the number of horses, which had sunk to just 30, be bolstered. The faithful staff that stayed on despite lucrative offers abroad were few in number: Chief Rider Gottlieb Polak, Ernst Lindenbauer, Alfred Cerha, Moritz Herold, Hermann Lippert, Johann Neumayr and Wenzel Zrust.

Performances in the Winter Riding School, now only held publicly, took on a new novelty – the principle "art for art's sake", which had been the backbone of the exclusive institute was now dispensed with. A constant, multi-faceted programme that needed to impress a larger audience not educated in the airs and technique had to be assembled with suitable music. The new road shows were also a challenge for the horses and riders. In the first few years the riding school performed in Berlin (1925), Aachen and London (1927), Den Haag (1928) and Brussels (1932), with a second trip to London in 1935. The Spanish Riding School became a symbol for the new Republic, and thus began the rise of worldwide fame for the school and its horses.

Above: Emperor Franz Joseph mounted during a manoeuvre. Painting by Julius von Blaas, 1898.
Left page: Colonel Alois Podhajsky, commander and director of the Spanish Riding School. Painting by Siegfried Stoitzner, 1952.

Above left: Stablemaster Prince Pallfy, 1918. Etching by Ludwig Michalek.
Above right: Count Rudolf van der Straten with his team. Photo ca. 1920.
Below: Count Rudolf van der Straten, director of the Spanish Riding School from 1920–1939, on a Lipizzan. Painting by Ludwig Koch, 1934.
Right page: The Winter Riding School during World War II.

THE LIPIZZANS IN WORLD WAR II – THE RESCUE OPERATION OF 1945

After Austria's annexation to the Third Reich in March 1938 the stud in Piber passed to the Ministry of Agriculture in Berlin, and the Spanish Riding School to the German High Command. Graf van der Straten resigned and nominated as his successor Colonel Alois Podhajsky, who had also been an official of the Dragoons in the imperial army and also had experience in the Spanish Riding School and with horses, particularly as an officer in the Austrian army and as commander of the Military Institute of Equitation and Driving. As well, Podhajsky had had a successful career as a competitor in international riding competitions, culminating in his victory at the European dressage championships (Budapest 1935)

and the Bronze medal won at the Olympic Games in 1936 in Berlin for Austria. Podhajsky took over as director of the Spanish Riding School on 1 June 1939; due to the military hierarchy he received the title of "Commander". His work was soon complicated by political pressure and then by the threat of war. Podhajsky managed to find a refuge for the school stallions in the Lainzer Tiergarten, a former hunting area, more specifically in the stables of the Hermesvilla, built by Emperor Franz Joseph I for Empress Elisabeth. Here the horses were protected from the shelling. Until recently the school's stallions spent the summer there; today their summer quarters are in Klein Wetzdorf in Lower Austria. For political reasons the riding school wasn't evacuated until February 1945. Colonel Podhajsky found refuge in the castle belonging to Count Arco in St. Martin near Schärding in Upper Austria. In the meantime, all the horses from the Piber stud had been transferred to Hostau in the Böhmerwald to a former Czech farm, which was also under German command and run by Lieutenant Colonel Hubert Rudofsky, an important equine expert. Dr. Rudolf Lessing from Berlin was also working as a veterinarian in Hostau, which at that time

housed over 100 of the best Arabians from Europe, more than 200 racing horses as well as 600 Cossack horses seized by the German armed forces. The numbers of the former Austrian Lipizzan herd increased due to additions from the Yugoslav imperial stud farms and private studs and from the main Italian stud farm in Lipizza, which had also been moved to Hostau. Many breeding possibilities arose during this time – though the results were disputed by specialists. In any case the horses were safe, and they prospered.

The fall of the German armed forces was nigh and it was feared that Hostau would be occupied by Russian troupes, which would probably destroy the stud. Because of this, the entire stud farm – more than 1000 animals – was secretly handed over to the American army, which had advanced into Bavaria. At the end of April, Rudofsky and other German officers had taken up contact with the 8th platoon of the US army, whose commander General George S. Patton, had been a dressage rider and had ridden in the 1912 Olympic Games in Stockholm. The amazing feat was coordinated by Colonel Charles H. Reed of the Second Cavalry Brigade. At the beginning of May almost all of the Austrian, Italian and Yugoslavian Lipizzans, 215 horses in total, were returned by the Americans to Podhajsky, who wasn't able to find room for all the horses in St. Martin and had to find other alternatives in Upper Austria. On the occasion of a show at the Spanish Riding School in honour of General Patton Podhajsky put the Lipizzans under the protection of the US army, thereby ensuring their continued existence. And that was how the American officers saved both institutions, the stud and the school, from extinction.

The stud remained in Wimsbach near Wels (Upper Austria) until it was moved to Piber in stages in 1952. The rest of the horses from Hostau ended up in German studs and were partly seized by the American army and taken to the States. In 1947 the Lipizzans that had been brought from Lipizza to Hostau were taken back to Italy. Breeding there wasn't intended, but soon a stud was opened in Piedmont in the Sabiner mountains north of Rome and breeding of riding and sport horses began. Yugoslavia on the other hand took the city of Triest and its hinterland with its stud farm Lipizza, which communist partisans had captured in 1944, but no longer had any horses. With Lipizzans from the stud in Demir Kapia and using seized noble and ecclesiastic studs, Yugoslavia resumed breeding in the newly named "Lipica" stud.

Above and centre: Moving the school stallions from the Stallburg to the Hermesvilla in the Lainzer Tiergarten due to the threat of bombing, 1943.
Below: Colonel Podhajsky handing over the riding school at the end of a performance in St. Martin am Inn to the protection of the 8th US Army and General George S. Patton, 7th May 1945.
Right page: *Capriole* on the reins, 1955.

THE SPANISH RIDING SCHOOL
IN THE SECOND REPUBLIC

The Riding School was henceforth located in Upper Austria and was confronted with the economic problems related to the aftermath of the war. How should the horses be taken care of in comparison to people? And based on this question, a return to Vienna was unthinkable. There was also the danger that the Riding School would be seized by the Russians since it had been a former institution of the German armed forces, and that Podhajsky, as former German officer, would be arrested. Following Podhajsky's agreement with the American occupying forces to return the original Lipizzans to Italy and those from Demir Kapia to Yugoslavia, the problems of care-taking and space were noticeably relieved. Podhajsky and his excellent staff of Chief Riders and Riders could now fully focus their attention on the actual task of preserving the Haute École of dressage riding. Regular performances took place in the former Dragoons post in Wels, and the period "in exile" was a very fruitful one for the school. From 1948 onwards the white stallions celebrated triumphs on tours throughout Europe; in 1950 they toured the USA for the first time. Only after the signing of the Austrian State Treaty did the Spanish Riding School return to the imperial palace in Vienna. After a hiatus of over a decade, the first performance in the Winter Riding School took place on 26 October 1955 as a ceremonious state celebration.

In 1964, just before retiring, Podhajsky took the school on a huge tour once again to the USA. The road show was meant as a thank you to the US army for saving the Riding School. Podhajsky received much adulation for having dedicated his life to equitation and a quarter of a century to the Spanish Riding School. With his enthusiasm and responsibility for his assigned task, he is rightly considered the saviour of an Austrian institution that has maintained its cultivated, century-old art of equitation despite the threats of mass tourism and related kitsch. This has also secured him an internationally sound reputation.

In 1965 Podhajsky was succeeded by Colonel Hans Handler, an excellent rider who had spent several years working at the riding school. In September 1972 it was decided that the 400th anniversary of the Spanish Riding School should be celebrated with splendid performances in the Winter Riding School, in the park at Schloss Schönbrunn and in the Vienna Stadthalle. The Riding School had already been founded in 1560, but due to a wrongly-read receipt related to construction work, the general date was falsely thought to be 1572. The celebrations drew illustrious guests from all over the world of horses: Saumur's *cadre noir*, the best team from the family of Domecq de Jerez, and white Kladruby horses as teams for the classic imperial gala coaches from Schönbrunn's *Wagenburg*.

Colonel Handler was succeeded by Kurt Albrecht, who fought vehemently against the increasing lack of comprehension from the public and authorities and especially with the bureaucracy involved in the activities and standards of the Spanish Riding School, and protected it against the demands of the world of tourism. In 1985 he retired as Brigadier General. At the same time the long-time director of the stud in Piber, Dr. Heinrich Lehrner, an important man in equitation, also retired. An epidemic that killed numerous mares and foals overshadowed Lehrner's last year as director, whereupon a new system was introduced which united the directorship of the stud with that of the Spanish Riding School. This task was given to the veterinary surgeon Dr. Jaromir Oulehla, whose primary goal was to re-establish a solid breeding foundation. Through Oulehla the Lipizzan Museum was founded in conjunction with the Kunsthistorisches Museum and was opened in December 1997. Following lengthy discussions about the traditional tasks and

future activities of the Riding School, the school and the stud in Piber became a private company on 1 January 2001 but nevertheless remained the property of the Austrian Republic.

Veterinarian and equine expert Dr. Werner Pohl became director of the new organisation "Spanish Riding School – Federal Stud Piber". In a very short time Pohl had transformed the school into a modern institution open to the world; he initiated extensive renovations in Piber, the Hofburg and in the stables, which fulfilled modern animal right's criteria. In 2005 Pohl was succeeded by Magister Armin Aigner, who was given the task of balancing the books at the stud and the Riding School.

The stud and the breeding of these priceless horses seems today to be on solid footing. But sometimes catastrophes can drop out of the sky: On 27 November 1992 a fire broke out in the Redoutensälen of the Hofburg, which threatened the National Library and the Winter Riding School. The Stallburg was not endangered, but the horses, spooked by the smoke and the noise, had to be taken from their stables and brought to safety. But they escaped onto the streets, and were captured and calmed by passers-by and taken to the Volksgarten where they trampled the lawns and flowerbeds.

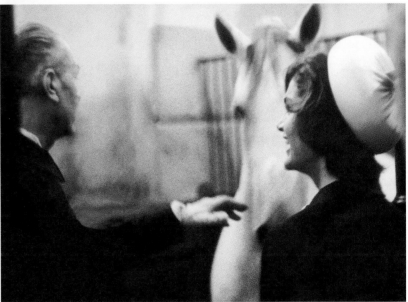

Above: Colonel Podhajsky with Maestoso Mercurio, 1955.
Centre: Colonel Podhajsky leading "Jackie", wife of John F. Kennedy, President of the United States, to the stallions in the stables.
Below: *Pas de Trois* on tournament grounds
Left page: Colonel Podhajsky with Siglavy Brezovica in a *courbette* on the rein, 1955.

Above: The 400th anniversary of the Spanish Riding School in 1972. Performance at Schloss Schönbrunn.
Below left: Chief Rider Ignaz Lauscha. *Courbette* on Siglavy Flora on tour in Nuremberg, 1979.
Centre right: *Ballotade* on the rein in Wembley Stadium in London, 1985.
Below right: Lipizzans on tour – Colonel Podhajsky leading a school horse out of the freight hold of an aeroplane.

Above left: School horses in their summer quarters in the Hermesvilla in Lainzer Tiergarten
Above right: Colonel Handler heading a team in the Winter Riding School
Below: Chief Rider and Rider greeting the portrait of the contractor, Emperor Charles VI, hanging in the imperial box at the Winter Riding School.

Piber:
The world of Lipizzans

HOME OF THE WHITE HORSES

Like almost all other important cultural or scientific institutions – opera and theatre, universities and academies, libraries and museums – the Austrian Lipizzan stud was financed and governed by the Austrian Empire; duties, which the State and its authorities took over in the 20th century. In recent years, however, the Austrian government, like other European states as well, began to withdraw from these institutions and therewith to dispose of one of its most important cultural duties. The Riding School in Vienna and the Lipizzan stud in Piber were privatised, with the definitive goal of becoming independent of state financing. In order to achieve this goal – mainly in the stud – major organisational and structural changes had to be made. Public interest for the character and running of the stud had to be drawn to attract more visitors than before. In this light, the Piber stud today presents itself as the "Home of the Lipizzans". Those living near and around Piber, in west Styria and in the capital city of Graz, should be aware that the world famous white horses are born and raised in their homeland – that they are in a way "Styrian".

The stud in Piber is also one of the centres of Lipizzan breeding, is fighting for its position as the most important centre, and therefore should – or must – be able to determine the definitive criteria for the unadulterated maintenance of the breed. Essentially, breeding in Piber must always have as its most important goal to provide the most noble, most talented and healthiest stallions for the

Above: A mother mare in front of the stables at Piber
Left page and following double page: The summer months are spent on mountain pastures at 1500 metres above sea level. Here the young Lipizzans develop their gait and sure-footedness. Their natural gait is later trained and developed at the school.

Haute École in Vienna and also to guarantee the broadest foundation for the oldest of Europe's breed of cultural horses. This challenge and objective has to be brought across to the Austrian public as well as be in accordance with other Lipizzan studs like Lipica in Slovenia, Topol'-cianky in Slovakia, Szilvásvárad in Hungary, Dakovo in Croatia and Monterotondo near Rome.

The beginning of the modern presentation of the Piber Federal Stud took place in 2003 at the Styrian provincial exhibition "The Myth of the Horse" at the Baroque castle in Piber and made the stud and its idyllic environment widely known to the public. Since then, tourism and gastronomy have improved and, most importantly, a hippodrome with public seating was built. Numerous horse and stud fêtes, horse and riding championships and other sports events take place here and have even attracted international visitors.

As well, a ceremonious appointment of recruits to the Austrian army took place in July 2006 – where light and heavy equipment was presented under the motto "Horse power in the army" – and drew the attention of the public.

The "World of Lipizzans" is also supposed to be a place that not only draws specialists or horse lovers but also laypeople – families with children and their friends - and where an exciting, information-packed day can be spent. Daily tours of the stud are offered giving visitors the opportunity to see new-born foals, witness mares and their foals running around in their pens or visit the horse-smith and find out about other Lipizzan-related topics. On certain days carriage rides are offered; riding and driving lessons can also be made by appointment. A visit to Piber is a worthwhile experience.

Epilogue

THE SPANISH RIDING SCHOOL TODAY

The Spanish Riding School directs our attention in a specific way to the special relationship between humans and the horse, between horse and rider. There are so many areas and periods of life in which this relationship plays a role, but where it takes different forms. In any case, the horse's ability to learn and to reproduce what it has learned through training has constantly fascinated humans and has made it possible to train the horse as our most important aid and companion.

The work place is where, for centuries, the horse has played an important role and still does. It has also been essential as the hunter's, the merchant's, the courier's mount; indispensable in the world of rulers, the military and police in which it was ridden by officers and representatives of the law, and beyond that, there is the wide, seemingly unrelated world of sport and entertainment such as the circus, which occupies a special place between both. In the circus, the horse is  the reliable partner of the athlete and the acrobat, and takes a back seat to their impressive feats. Or it becomes part of a group and is presented as the teachable and clever animal. As producers of the perfectly coordinated show, we often become blasé about the actual abilities of the animal, acting as the forcing power, the more powerful partner in the relationship between the two beings. In sport the relationship between horse and rider is very personal and close, and the horse isn't only trained by the rider in order to achieve the particular goal – the goal is to win: the horse wants to lead the race, jump the hurdle, and the victory his shared by both horse and the rider. Both parties are equal.

The long historical tradition in the Spanish Riding School, its anachronistic presence, its independence from competition, sensationalism and fashionable entertainment all show the perhaps most extreme variation of this relationship. The goal of harmony between rider and horse is the highest priority at the institute – and is also attained. It is no wonder that the term "horsemanship" is used. Art, as shown by the great philosophers of the 18th century, exists for itself in its own right, outside the realms of purpose and use. In its uniqueness and its particular character, the idea of the artistic end-in-itself opens a new outlook on the entire art-historical relationship regarding man and horse. Using their respective means, the Viennese Lipizzan Museum and the author of this guide have taken it upon themselves to direct and reflect on this outlook and bring it to the broader public.

Above: Each stall carries a plaque with the name of the father (sire stallion Neapolitano) and the mother (Biserka) and the year of birth.
Left page: First Chief Rider Klaus Krzisch on Siglavy Mantua I.
Next double page: Large school quadrille, the unforgettable finale of a Riding School performance.

Photographs
Illustrations/photos of Lipizzan Museum objects from the Kunsthistorisches Museum Vienna:
7, 8/9, 10, 11, 14, 15, 16, 26, 27, 30/31, 44 (above), 46
Spanish Riding School (Photos by Peter Rigaud and Herbert Graf): Front cover, 1, 2/3, 4, 19, 20, 21, 22, 23, 28, 29, 32, 33, 34, 35, 36 (centre right and below), 39, 55, 56, 57, 58/59, 60, 61, 62, 63
Lipizzan Museum: 17, 18, 24, 36 (left half of picture and above right), 37, 38 (right), 48, 49, 50, 51, 52, 53, 54
Kunsthistorisches Museum: Back cover, 6, 12/13, 25, 38 (left), 40, 41, 42, 43, 44 (below), 45, 47
British Museum, London: 5
APA-Grafik: 8
Pichler Verlag: 9 (below)

The Author
Georg Kugler worked in the Kunsthistorisches Museum library from 1959 and in the Wagenburg at Schönbrunn, where he was director from 1973 to 2000. In 1990 he became assistant general director of the Kunsthistorisches Museum. Currently, Kugler is scientific director of the Lipizzan Musuem, and through numerous publications has become a leading authority on Viennese and Austrian cultural history. Included in his oeuvre is the major work *Die Lipizzaner der Spanischen Hofreitschule* (with W. Bihl) published in 2002.

ISBN 978-3-85431-415-8

Author: Georg Kugler
Book and cover design: Bruno Wegscheider
Graphics and layout: Franz Hanns
Translation: Mý Huê McGowran

Reproduction: Pixelstorm, Vienna
Printing and binding: Dimograf, Bielsko-Biała, Poland